PURE-OGRAPHY

A 14-day journey of purifying your mind.
Release the Mental Weight and Receive Mental Freedom

Become the driver of your thoughts. Don't just be a passenger; steer yourself on the journey of wholeness.

MIRIAM MATTHEWS

Copyright

Table of Contents

Introduction

Have you ever found yourself wondering, "Why do I think this way?" or "Why is it hard for me to change?" Do you struggle with knowing your worth, fear, or letting go of past pain?

Some of us often find ourselves struggling with thoughts that we don't even want to think about. Some of us are also holding on to past hurts and traumas that lead us to feel fearful, insecure, resentful, and angry, just to name a few. With every experience, we acquire a new belief. Some beliefs can be helpful, and others can become harmful. Due to our human nature, there's also a tendency to reflect on and meditate on the negative events that have transpired throughout our lives.

Everyone has experienced a negative event in life. However, negative beliefs that arise from these experiences should not hinder your growth and become a barrier to living life abundantly.

One of the most googled questions is, "Can I change?" The answer is yes, and you know when you're ready to change.

I was born in Atlanta, GA, and grew up with a single mother who worked hard to care for us. Despite her efforts, we still faced constant financial difficulties. Additionally, I experienced sexual trauma and bullying, which led me to develop negative beliefs about myself. Seeking the approval of others became a constant in my life, and I struggled with anxiety in group settings and with speaking in public.

I battled negative thoughts daily, grappling with impostor syndrome that plagued my mind. More often than not, my mind would wander, and I'd go with the flow of the thoughts, no matter how negative they were. Unfortunately, how I saw myself on the inside is what I reflected on the outside.

I experienced many bad relationships and then became pregnant in college. After having my first child, as a single mother, I realized the cycle was repeating. I finally decided enough was enough and made up my mind that I was ready for change. I developed my relationship with God and got the help I needed.

I am now a 3x bestselling author and international best-selling author as well as a therapist and coach with two successful businesses and multiple streams of income. Shifting my perspective transformed my pain into a powerful purpose, one that has been profitable and impactful. Today, I am privileged to speak on multiple public platforms about winning the battle of the mind!

My mission is to help people master their mindsets, and walk in power and purpose by truly understanding the DNA they carry! The results and testimonials from those I've helped speak for themselves.

If you want your circumstances to change, it all starts with changing your mindset. You have been in a battle. It's the battle of the mind. Whether you show up for the battle or hide, the battle will go on. However, the truth is that you're not meant to hide. You are meant to show up, win, and break the mental chains that have held you down! It's time to break out of those generational cycles of negative beliefs and poverty, as you ARE THE GENERATIONAL BREAKER for your family and community.

To attain something you've never had before, you have to be willing to do something you have never done before. It doesn't matter what limiting beliefs you have or how long you've had those beliefs about yourself; it is your time to change them!

Change requires intention and is often best achieved with support and accountability. If the connections you've had for years are in a similar cycle you are struggling to break from, it's definitely worth connecting with those who are where you want to go. Have you ever wondered why? It's because chances are these current connections are grappling with the same negative beliefs, which is why you are in the same cycle. The most efficient and wise way is to connect with someone who has already achieved what you aspire to achieve. That's why I encourage you to book a complimentary discovery call with me. You can do so at bonus.defineyourdna.com!

By purchasing this book, you are connecting yourself to someone who has transcended the cycle, and it will help you step out of whatever cycle you have been in. Proverbs 23:7 reminds us, "For as a person thinks in his heart, so is he." That means that you are responsible for what you think. What we think is what settles into our hearts.

It's with our hearts that we oftentimes make decisions. These decisions can either propel us toward success or create issues in our lives that have detrimental consequences. Therefore, it is essential to be mindful of your thoughts because you are always driving somewhere.

Now ask yourself, "Am I driving towards my purpose or away from it?" The answer lies under the hood (your mind) of the car. The car has been through a lot. It has endured bumps and collisions and perhaps other people have driven it sometimes, or you have taken direction from others thinking that you'd get to the intended destination. However, instead, you got lost and now feel fearful, lonely, maybe frustrated, and angry.

This book is absolutely transformative and your transformation can be enhanced by implementing these considerations. It will help bring awareness to the mental battles you are experiencing and will take you through a journey of understanding and purification while leading you to see yourself and your circumstances from a different perspective. Throughout its pages, you will be taken through a process of defining your DNA.

Dive into God. Neutralize negative beliefs. Activate Power and Purpose. You were made to stand out and make an impact with your God-given gifts. Often, we allow past experiences and pain to lead us to believe that we are not good enough or instill fear that holds us from fulfilling our purpose. But remember, your past is your push for your purpose!

Considerations

1. Consider fasting over the next 14 days. The fast can be a water fast, a fast with smoothies, or a fast with fruits and vegetables (This is not medical advice Consult your physician if necessary).
2. Refrain from engaging in any social media, television/reality shows/movies, pornographic material, or content on the Internet or in books and magazines that may hinder your growth.
3. Avoid listening to any music that is degrading or sad. Instead, create a playlist that glorifies God and uplifts your spirit.
4. Be intentional about avoiding negative conversations, such as gossip. If there are individuals with whom you usually engage in this type of conversation, separate yourself from them for the next two weeks. You can simply explain that you are doing a mental cleanse for clarity and personal growth, without going into detail if you do not want to.

Consider inviting someone to join you on this journey. Accountability and support can be incredibly beneficial in remaining committed to the end. Sharing this book with someone else may also provide them the freedom that they need and have been longing for.

Instructions

This book contains exercises, affirmations, and visualizations designed to empower and transform you. I encourage you to be as open and transparent with yourself as possible. Commit to completing each and every exercise along with all of the affirmations. Even if it feels difficult, do the affirmations in front of the mirror. Some individuals report challenges with looking at themselves in the mirror and saying affirmations, but doing so can significantly amplify the results.

Before engaging in the visualizations, take the time to read through them thoroughly. Set a timer for about 5 minutes during your visualizations. If you'd prefer to be guided during your visualizations, you can listen to the audio version by accessing them at this link: bonus.pure-ography.com.

As you begin this book, say this prayer, "God, please help me to shift the way I perceive myself so that my perception aligns with your view of me. Help me to shift my thinking so that my beliefs and thoughts align with who you say I am. Please remove any hardened aspects of my heart and give me a pure heart. Grant me a teachable spirit and remove every veil of deception so that I can develop into the person you have called me to be. In Jesus' name, Amen."

Now, you are ready to discover the DNA within you so that you can walk the path Christ has set for you.

Chapter 1
Rejection

Who have you anchored your self-worth to?

"I just want to be accepted," is a statement that hundreds of my clients have expressed at the beginning of their journey of healing. According to the Goodreads therapeutic journal, rejection most frequently refers to the feelings of shame, sadness, or grief people feel when they are not accepted by others.

The American Psychological Association has also found a correlation between the pain of rejection and physical pain. A researcher, following his personal experience of being excluded by frisbee players at the park, developed an online game called cyberball with his team of researchers.

He used an MRI scanner to determine how rejection reveals itself in the brain. In cyberball, the subject plays an online game of catch with two other players.

Eventually, the two other players start throwing the ball only to each other, excluding the subject.

Compared with the volunteers who continue to be included, those who are rejected show increased activity in the dorsal anterior cingulate and anterior insula, two parts of the brain that show increased activity and response to physical pain. In other words, as far as your brain is concerned, a broken heart is no different from a broken arm. Astonishing, isn't it?

Many of us can relate to childhood experiences of not being picked for a team or a game and feeling rejected. It didn't feel good at all. Many of us have experienced some sort of challenge or trauma.

The human brain is designed to register that trauma to ensure that it doesn't happen again. This registration acts as a reminder. The brain sends notifications of negativity, like a phone sends alerts, reminding us of past hurts. Alert: "You weren't picked." Alert: "You're not their choice." Alert: "It's better to be alone and avoid people." It is essentially activating a defense mechanism to help keep you safe. However, this doesn't mean that we've healed from the hurt. In addition to this, with every experience, a belief is created.

One of the most common beliefs is the belief of not being good enough. This belief is birthed out of a bad experience. Even though you are not bad, whatever you behold to be true in your mind can create a sense of bereavement in your heart, similar to the "broken heart" referred to above. As stated earlier, a broken heart is no different than a broken arm, according to your brain.

Perhaps you've felt rejected as a result of divorce, family dynamics, broken friendships, a painful breakup, being stood up, being cheated on, losing a job, or not being chosen for a position you desired at some organization or even at church.

Additionally, many people fear rejection because pain does not feel good. Nevertheless, there is a remedy. You are not meant to view yourself from a distorted point of view based on an experience that you have had. Your true value isn't determined or diminished by others. Your value has been established since the beginning of time, and although you may have experienced pain, it is not meant for you to remain in pain but to be propelled towards your purpose.

Many individuals find themselves held back from pursuing their calling or purpose because they do not trust that they will be okay, no matter the challenges they face. However, I want to emphasize that all things are working together for your good. Truly, man's rejection is God's protection.

A wise peer of mine said, "It's not that you are a reject; it's that they didn't have the capacity to see your value." Oftentimes, we waste time trying to make sense of why we're not liked or accepted when it truly doesn't make sense. And if their rejection of you doesn't make sense, why allow their "senseless" view of you to define how you see yourself? It doesn't make sense!

This also means that there is something better in store for you; allow the remedy of God's possibility to overshadow and remove the pain that is in your heart. Just like a broken arm needs repair, your heart needs healing and it's time for it to be healed. The way to do that is by removing and replacing the thoughts in your mind.

Let's begin by exposing the negative experiences and beliefs. Write about an experience where you felt rejected, and describe the negative beliefs you acquired as a result.

Negative Experiences where I felt rejected

____

____

____

____

____

____

Negative Beliefs

____

____

____

____

____

____

____

All things work together for the good of those who love God and are called according to His purpose. (Romans 8:28)

It's time for your visualization. Visualizations are very important as you are intentionally giving your mind new information. New information requires new associative visions. If you can see it, you are reprogramming your thinking.

Recall what you wrote above, as you'll use it below. Before continuing, grab a picture of yourself at around the age of seven. Take a moment to look at the picture and capture it in your mind. Now let's begin the visualization:

Visit **https://bonus.pure-ography.com/** to listen to the audio visualization.

Visualization

God tells you that you are His child, so He wants you to visualize yourself in a childlike form. You begin to see yourself as a 7-year-old. Now picture yourself sitting on God's lap. He lovingly tells you that it's time to recognize your value and He wants to show you a movie about your life.

You suddenly cover your eyes, but He gently pulls your hands down and says "It's okay. You need to see it." In this movie, He shows you what was happening behind the scenes of the rejection story. For people who rejected you, picture their eyes being covered, indicating they didn't have the capacity to see your value. Because of their limited capacity, they wouldn't have been able to sustain a healthy relationship with you or anyone else for that matter.

For places that rejected you, you begin to see the entry being blocked because God's hand was redirecting you elsewhere. On the other side of His hand, you see a situation that didn't match the standard He would have wanted for you. See how every rejection or block was a push for you to recognize your value in Him. It was a push towards something better and prosperous. "Now I see," you exclaim.

You get off His lap, and return to your current age. However, you're not the same because you are now able to see your value.

Everything was working together for your good. Jesus is the way, the truth, and the life. Following His way is the key to knowing your worth. As a result, instead of rejection, you now have direction, and you have placed the anchor of your self-worth in Him. See yourself smiling again. He tells you to go forward into the bigger and better things that He has for you. Now see yourself walking with certainty!

You are now the gardener of your life, uprooting the weeds of negative belief and planting new seeds of self-worth and confidence. It's time to plant new seeds. Let's recite these affirmations with conviction!

Grab your mirror. It's time for affirmations.

- I am willing to view life differently.
- I am willing to view myself differently.
- All things are working together for my good.
- I am not too much for God to handle.

- I am respected and respectful.
- I am fearfully and wonderfully made.
- I am treasured by the one true King.
- I am protected by God.
- I am made for an intended purpose.
- My value isn't determined by mankind.
- God thought about me when He made the heavens and the earth.
- I have always been a part of His plan and purpose.
- God's love for me removes the pain, and I am restored today.
- I am loved by the one whose love is perfect.
- I am courageously walking into uncharted places because God is with me.
- I am not alone.
- My steps are ordered by God!

Chapter 2
Burdens

His yoke is easy and His burden is light. Matthew 11:30

A burden is typically defined as the emotional stress that you may experience as a result of your capacity being too full. This often arises from the magnitude of responsibility you are assigned or take on. It can also result from the overextension of oneself—not only managing your own responsibilities and emotions but also making other people's responsibilities and emotions your responsibility as well.

Why do we do this? We do this because we care. However, empathy without boundaries can lead to the disempowerment of others and render us vulnerable to exploitation and burnout. This leads us towards exploitation and burnout. Sometimes, this pattern arises from guilt from the past or rules that you adopted in childhood.

I've spoken with people who, due to inadequate supervision in their home, began taking care of their siblings at a very young age. A parent who wasn't present assigned that role to them.

You may have even experienced taking on the role of a comforter for a sibling or even a parent, which led to a codependent relationship where there is reliance on you even in adulthood. Or perhaps there was emotional neglect, which made you feel unattended or uncared for in childhood and as a result, you may have developed an extreme of overcompensating for others so they don't feel as you did in childhood.

This may lead to a tendency to overextend oneself to others. For instance, a parent can overextend themselves to their adult children with the intention of helping them but inadvertently enabling them, which can prove harmful. Another example could be taking on more responsibilities in a marriage to avoid conflict or confrontation. In a work setting, this might manifest as a challenge with delegation or reluctance to ask for help, leading to an increased workload.

I remember being taught a scripture that read, "I will not put too much on you than you can bear." Yet, the full scripture says more. "No temptation has seized you except what is common to man, and God is faithful; he will not let you be tempted beyond what you can bear. But when you are tempted, he will also provide a way out so that you can stand up under it." (1 Corinthians 10:13) Temptation is a desire to do something, especially something wrong or unwise. Giving in to temptation results in compromising values, instead of allowing for cultivation or growth.

Therefore, it may be tempting to respond to someone's need for help out of emotion, but if decisions are made without wisdom, we can end up doing more harm than good. It could be tempting to stick with the familiar childhood roles, even in your adulthood because change seems daunting.

It can be tempting to maintain a certain role in someone's life because you don't want to disappoint them.It can be tempting to take on certain burdens because you've associated your value with how you show up in people's lives. It can be tempting to enable someone's bad behavior and allow a co-dependent relationship because their dependence on you fulfills some type of internal need.

It can also be tempting to keep saying yes even when you are overextended because you want to avoid conflict. But, remember, God's burden is easy and His yoke is light. (Matthew 11:30) This scripture suggests two things: not every burden comes from God, and when God gives us a heavy assignment, it's not because He was expecting us to do it by ourselves. You can count on His divine strength.

Many people, especially Christians, struggle to differentiate between serving others and people-pleasing. The burnout that I'm referring to comes from people-pleasing and not allowing God's spirit to refresh you and reveal to you the changes that need to be made as you're dealing with people, ministry, family, work, and so on.

People-pleasing can stem from a lack of boundaries, which leads to self-assigned roles. You then end up always striving to do the work that others actually need to do to achieve their own growth and prosperity. This is like clocking in at work under their name and then giving them the paycheck. If this happens, they won't learn or acquire the skills or experiences needed to sustain the job.

When you do the work that others need to do, they will not learn and will continue to depend on you. I'm not saying that no one should be able to lean on you; however, leaning is meant to be temporary. It is not meant for you to carry your own cross as well as theirs.

God is the source for everyone, and as we look to Him, He gives us all guidance and supernatural strength to help each and every one of us with life and with our assignments. Our capacities for serving others differ from person to person.

Remember, people-pleasing arises from associating your value or worth with the position or role that you have in someone's life while aiming to maintain their stability or peace of mind. It can also come from fear of not wanting to disappoint them, which is also correlated with how you see yourself and how you want others to see you. When you truly assess this, you'll realize that the only person who can take on the burdens of all people perfectly is God, and for Him, it is not burdensome. He does this for all of us.

This new revelation will reveal to you the relationships where you have overextended yourself so you can begin shedding the mental weight. It's time for a role adjustment!

It's time to expose the negative beliefs. Take some time to list the negative beliefs that have kept you in codependent relationships or have resulted in you shouldering burdens. Alternatively, you can reflect on the effects of taking this role. For instance, a negative belief (lie) I've told myself might be: "Even though I know I shouldn't agree to this request, if I don't, the relationship will feel awkward and start to crumble, I can't bear the discomfort of disappointing someone."

Side Note: Even if there is a disappointment, who says it has to be awkward to say, "No, not this time" or "I'm unable to."? By exposing the lie, you are positioning yourself to see the truth. The truth being: "I am capable of handling whatever reaction may come." "It's perfectly okay for me to have boundaries, even if others initially resist them."

Now, begin to expose the lies or negative beliefs:

____

____

____

____

____

____

____

____

Who or what has become a burden in your life and why?

____

____

____

____

____

____

Visit **https://bonus.pure-ography.com**/ to listen to the audio visualization.

Visualization

(Reflect on your responses above.)

Envision yourself in a room with God. You have just consulted with Him, and He has refreshed you and given you the wisdom to perceive and navigate with clarity.

Picture a scale sitting on a table before you, representing your assignments as well as burdens that need to be discarded. In your meeting with God, He tells you to no longer fear the faces of men or women, or make yourself responsible for their outcome when you've done your part. He tells you that your purpose is to help people while pointing them back to Him. You have done your part and He will do the rest.

Prayer is your new position regarding that person, as the primary role has always been His. You begin to remove the burdens off the scale and as you do, the scale begins to balance out. Now, take a deep breath and release every weight with your breath. As you breathe out, focus on the thought, “I let go of this burden now.” You now feel as light as a feather, while reminding yourself that His yoke is easy and His burden is light.

Clarity Moment: What clarity and direction do you now have? (If needed, pray and ask God for direction, then repeat this visualization.)

Grab your mirror. It's time for affirmations.

- You have now positioned yourself to see and speak the truth:
- God is my source and everyone else's as well.
- I am not alone, for He is my guide.
- I am giving myself permission to discard the burdens that I have taken upon myself.
- I'm giving myself permission to step out of the roles that were not meant for me.
- It's okay for me to ask for help.
- I let go of the guilt from the past.
- I am willing to change.
- I’m giving others the space and time to learn their own lessons.
- My value isn't diminished by somebody's disappointment in me.

- I'm willing to learn and let go of the inner judgments and criticism.
- We are all here to learn lessons and our lessons empower us.
- As long as I reflect the nature of Christ, my peace is not contingent upon someone being happy with me.
- I am allowing myself to be transparent.
- It is beneficial for me and others to have boundaries.
- I respect my "no," as well as the "no" of others as well.
- It's okay for me to let go of the roles that I have assigned myself.
- God is my source and the source for others as well.

A special note from Coach Miriam

You have been empowered to make the necessary changes. You have now come into agreement with the truth that your value doesn't diminish or isn't altered based on someone's behavior. You understand that boundaries are crucial for your protection and for the empowerment of others.

Your implementation of that boundary isn't a weapon, and you don't have to worry about their reaction to your boundary—good or bad. Their reaction to your boundary isn't as important as the outcome of your boundary, which will yield empowerment. Empowerment offers both you and them a chance to learn and grow. So yes, you are feeling empowered.

Challenge: Set one boundary this week. What is the boundary and with whom are you going to establish it?

Boundary	With

Chapter 3
Anger

"Emotions buried alive don't die; they accumulate"-Anonymous

"I'm angry, I'm upset, I'm frustrated, I'm irritated." Anger is an emotion that all of us have. God created us with emotions, but we are not meant to be controlled by them.

Often, anger is a byproduct of unmet needs or unresolved issues that have built up over time. Then, like a volcano, there is an emotional eruption of feelings, depleting the individual and potentially causing harm to oneself as well as others.

Many people that I have spoken to agree that the emotion of anger doesn't appear suddenly; it is built over time. I have learned that anytime you are looking at someone who's angry, you're actually looking at someone who is feeling a lack of love and appreciation. However, many of us tend to meet anger with anger, irritation with irritation, and frustration with frustration.

We live in a time where we are inclined to become "triggered," a term we throw around as if to normalize that anyone can set you off with the push of a button.

This shouldn't be the case. Webster's Dictionary defines “trigger” as a mechanism that actuates a ranged weapon such as a firearm, airgun, crossbow, or speargun. The word may also be used to describe a switch that initiates the operation of other non-shooting devices such as a trap, a power tool, or a quick release.

By allowing yourself to be “triggered,” you are coming into agreement that your emotions are bullets and that you can turn into a weapon at the push of the wrong button. There's a scripture that speaks to this: “For the weapons of our warfare are not carnal but mighty in God for pulling down strongholds.” (2 Corinthians 10:4). “Carnal” refers to belief systems that you have developed and abide by as a result of your upbringing and culture. This doesn't mean that every belief system is wrong.

Still, maybe you have seen conflict resolution mishandled growing up. Perhaps you may have witnessed domestic violence at home, encompassing not only emotional abuse but physical abuse as well. Maybe you have experienced some form of mistreatment or violation that you have not completely healed.

You could have grown up around individuals who are emotionally stifled or lack emotional maturity and don't readily take accountability for their mistakes. As a result, you may have seen them constantly blaming others, and those who live in that home are being accused or emotionally neglected. “Emotions buried alive do not die, they accumulate.” Anger is merely a symptom of what is going on underneath a wound.

You may see the outward explosion, but internally, there's a multitude of emotions and thoughts. No one is an innately angry person; they are instead individuals craving love and appreciation, even those whose anger you've experienced. Misunderstanding is one of the most significant, yet undiagnosed disorders that create dysfunction in relationships. How about making becoming trigger-proof your new normal?

Being trigger-proof means not having hidden bullets inside you, waiting to come out thus turning you into a weapon instantaneously. Again, I'm not saying anger is bad. Actually, anger can be used for good. A perfect example is Jesus becoming angry when the people had turned the church into a den of thieves by abusing the intended purpose of the church.

There is such a thing as holy anger. It shows the need for justice, or boundaries, and passion for the restoration of what has been exploited. In this instance, it can be a catalyst for purpose. However, what I'm referring to is something different.

The better you are at exploring your own feelings and communicating from a place of peace, the more acknowledged you will feel and the less you will allow anger to control you. We all want to feel validated and acknowledged. We all want to feel heard and understood. However, this doesn't solely depend on someone else acknowledging us; it starts with us acknowledging and understanding ourselves by exploring our emotions.

Some adults may use certain phrases such as, “I feel some type of way” or “I'm angry or upset,” not realizing that these are symptoms of emotional neglect or feelings of rejection or abandonment stemming from childhood. As a result, they may go from 0 to 10 and then communicate their feelings in a way that their words end up being weapons that cause more harm than good. This happens because they have not exercised emotional regulation and healthy communication.

Once you begin to explore your emotions, you can then rediscover your needs and begin to address them. Addressing your needs from a place of peace will yield a solution instead of a fight. It’s time to press P.A.U.S.E (Patience, Acknowledgment, Understanding, Symbolic, Explore) on anger, so you can find peace.

Now let's explore some of the beliefs that you've held that have constrained your ability to manage your emotions, resulting in instances of emotional immaturity and/or unhealthy communication in relationships. Examples of such beliefs include “I'm an angry person,” “I have to yell to be heard,” “Nobody will ever love me,” “Nobody will ever understand me,” “I will always be misunderstood,” and “Everyone is out to hurt me.”

Write down one to three triggers that have been directly associated with you becoming quickly irritated or angry. For instance, have the triggers been when someone has ignored you, disrespected you, or taken advantage of you? List them below.

____

____

____

____

____

____

Reflect on how one of these triggers has shown up lately. It could be in a marriage, a relationship with your child, a friend, your parents, a co-worker, a supervisor, a family member, a church member, or anyone else.

For example, Trigger: I become triggered when I'm ignored. Recent experience: I was recently ignored by my spouse when I was speaking to him. When I asked him to recall what I said, he wasn't paying attention and was busy texting on his phone. I became angry and yelled, "You never listen to me!" My spouse looked at me, astonished that I had become angry and was hurt by my words. We began to wonder why I was so quickly irritated.

Now you have connected the emotional trigger to a recent experience. What was the recent experience?

____

____

____

____

____

____

____

Visit https://bonus.pure-ography.com/ to listen to the audio visualization.

Visualization

Recall the recent experience you wrote about above. It's time for a redo of that moment. Picture yourself in the same setting with the same person or people. Whatever the trigger is that you identified, picture yourself feeling the emotion of anger rise. As you identify the trigger and feel the anger surge, PAUSE.

Notice your body and its reaction to you becoming angry. Now, picture Patience coming into you in the form of a white light. This visualization gives you the opportunity to acknowledge that you are upset and to understand why. In your understanding, you realize that this isn't the first time this has happened and that it is symbolic of a deeper issue. Then take time to explore the root of where it came from.

Next, picture a younger version of yourself, when you first began to feel this way—this is when the hurt first began. Imagine yourself standing in front of the younger you.

Give the younger you a hug. Tell them you see them, you acknowledge them and you love them. Tell them it will be okay. Now watch the younger you shrink until they fit into the palm of your hand and place them in your heart.

Now take a deep breath. Instead of anger, you now feel acknowledged. Now press PLAY, and watch yourself address your concern from a place of peace, resulting in a positive outcome. You did it!

Challenge: Try this once this week, and write about it here:

____

____

____

____

____

Grab your mirror. It's time for affirmations.

You have positioned yourself to see and speak the truth:

- I have power, love, and a sound mind.
- I am not too much for God to handle.
- I am willing to acknowledge my emotions and release them.
- I am God's precious child.
- I am understood by God.
- I am fearfully and wonderfully made.
- I communicate with love.
- Because God is in me, I am love.
- God is my source of love, and I share His love with others.

- Peace is an everyday experience for me.
- I am able to express myself in a healthy way.
- I am taking accountability for how I make myself feel.
- I am taking accountability for the words that I use and say.
- I am choosing to honor myself and others.
- I am able to speak with truth and grace.
- I am patient.
- I am slow to anger.
- I am solution-focused.
- I am choosing to build in every conversation, rather than tearing anyone down.

Chapter 4
Pride

"Pride goes before destruction, and a haughty spirit before a fall." Proverbs 16:18

"Pride" can be defined as the undue confidence in and attention to one's own skills, accomplishments, state, possessions, or position. The term "undue" represents extreme or inflated beliefs that one's intellect and experiences are the primary focus, overshadowing the perspectives and experiences of others.

Consequently, a prideful person may place more value on their viewpoints while simultaneously devaluing or invalidating the perspectives of others.

Pride can often be easier to recognize than to define, and it is typically simpler to recognize in others than in oneself. Some of the synonyms for pride may include arrogance, presumption, conceit, self-satisfaction, boasting, and high-mindedness.

Proverbs 16:18 warns us that pride comes before destruction. When referring to pride, I do not mean commending oneself or celebrating one's accomplishments and achievements. On the contrary, I am referring to the practice of being subjective, which means only looking at yourself and others from your point of view. This can lead you to think that your perspective or opinions are always right. As we learned from the previous chapter, someone who has an issue with pride doesn't develop overnight. This can be a learned behavior and often stems from earlier experiences that caused one pain.

Pain that is not healed or resolved can then turn into an idol that begins to consume your energy and focus. For instance, imagine being told that you're not good enough and internalizing that belief at a young age. For some people, that seed begins to take root in their hearts, and proving others wrong becomes their main focus.

Everything stemming from this mentality may seem good, as it drives you to achieve a degree, a nice job, or acquire a luxury car. However, while these achievements aren't inherently bad, they spring from a seed of pain that has not been uprooted and continues to inhabit your heart. Everything you do stems from pain or revenge, which transforms into pride and becomes the lens through which you view yourself and others.

I've spoken to many accomplished individuals who have made materialism their primary focus but are never at rest. They have confidence and are skillful, but they are restless and struggle with low self-esteem. They feel the constant need to achieve more or acquire materialistic things in order to feel good, but this never works and they wonder why they are not happy.

I've also seen situations where that same lens has led individuals to isolate themselves as they are constantly paranoid and skeptical about others or even consider themselves superior to others. These individuals often easily see other people's mistakes and issues, but rarely recognize their own errors. Time and time again, I've seen that, as a result of this, these individuals lack peace and there is sabotage in their relationships.

Relationships crumble because a prideful person can also be divisive, quickly cutting someone off as a defense mechanism, so that they don't experience that same pain rooted in past trauma. Even one's health and finances can be destroyed as a result of pride. Pride limits an individual's ability to have an enlightened or enlarged perspective because they've placed their beliefs and emotions on a pedestal that has essentially become their god.

The Bible highlights the importance of knowledge, understanding, and wisdom that go beyond the subjective mindset where a prideful person only prioritizes their perspective. "Buy truth, and do not sell it for love or money; buy wisdom, buy education, buy insight." (Proverbs 23:23, MSG) Knowledge will yield new information. Understanding will yield Vision Beyond how you've seen things because it allows for objectivity. Objectivity allows for empathy due to an enlarged perspective. Wisdom will facilitate application, which is a part of your transformation.

In this section, contemplate how adhering to a certain way of thinking has created sabotage or destruction in your life. Then write down the ways in which you have noticed Pride operating in your life. Example: "Pride has led me to want to always be right." "I find myself being very defensive and lacking empathy or objectivity in my relationships." "I find it difficult to say sorry when I'm wrong."

____
____
____
____
____
____
____
____
____
____

Let's begin with Prayer

Psalm 51:6 Says, "Behold, You desire truth in the inward parts, and in the hidden part, You will make me to know wisdom."

"The eyes of your understanding being enlightened; that ye may know what is the hope of his calling, and what the riches of the glory of his inheritance in the saints." (Ephesians 1:18)

These scriptures serve as an enlightening prayer and are key to unlocking the parts of you that need change even though you may not be aware of the specific changes that are needed because of how your perspective or thinking has been for many years.

Lord, please forgive me for being prideful. Help me to be teachable and humble. Put truth in the inward parts of me and wisdom in every hidden corner. I pray for the understanding that you want me to have, beyond my own reasoning. In Jesus' name, amen!

Visit **https://bonus.pure-ography.com/** to listen to the audio visualization.

Visualization

In this visualization, imagine yourself sitting in a chair at home. You have just asked God for truth to come into you and you've also asked Him for wisdom and understanding to enter you as well.

Suddenly His light begins to enter you and you begin to have an understanding and revelation that you didn't have before. It allows you to see yourself and others in a healthier way.

You begin to feel your defense mechanisms decreasing as you let go of the need to protect yourself by only being guided by your perspective. You are now allowing yourself to be guided by God's wisdom instead of your own.

You are cultivated by the healthy conviction of the Holy Spirit. As a result, you begin to let go of your assumptions about those with whom you have had misunderstandings and begin to see the possibility for change, redemption, and a healthy relationship. Not because you are imposing change on them but because you are welcoming accountability for yourself and your reactions. You are surrounded by light on the inside and outside. Before you open your eyes, visualize this light of truth staying with you everywhere you go.

Challenge: Think about a recent disagreement you had with someone that may have ended with a misunderstanding on both sides. Now that the light of truth is with you, try being objective and empathetic. Without placing blame on them or yourself, what can you now understand about them that you didn't before?

Grab your mirror. It's time for affirmations

- I am willing to change.
- I am ready to stop criticizing myself and others.
- I welcome the knowledge, understanding, and wisdom that God has for me.
- I acknowledge the different capacities that people have.
- I am teachable and I can learn.
- I am taking accountability for my actions.
- I am not too much for God to handle.
- I am committed to living life abundantly.

- I am open to new beginnings.
- I am not what happened to me; I am the resilience that rises above it.
- I am welcoming of new perspectives in my life.
- Peace is my portion.
- I am forgiving of others, and I extend grace and compassion to them.
- I choose to see the human side of people again.
- I recognize the value in myself and others.
- I choose humility and I am humble.

Chapter 5
Prisoner of Projecting

"For as he thinks in his heart, so is he." (Proverbs 23:7)

According to Karen R. Koenig, M.Ed. LCSW, projection refers to unconsciously taking unwanted emotions or traits you don't like about yourself, and attributing them to someone else or perceiving that others see you in the negative ways you see yourself. Think about a projector. It takes the inside picture or movie and displays it on the outside.

A common example is when an individual believes they are not good enough, at work, in a relationship, and so on. Instead of acknowledging their own belief system as the primary issue, they transfer, or project, this behavior onto others and focus on how they think others may perceive them.

Here are a few examples of distorted beliefs that an individual may hold, based on the terms and definitions from therapistaid.com:

Magnification or minimization: Exaggerating or minimizing the importance of events. One might believe their own achievements are unimportant, or that their mistakes are excessively important.

Catastrophizing: Seeing only the worst possible outcomes of a situation.

Magical thinking: The belief that acts will influence unrelated situations. For example, “I'm a good person, therefore bad things shouldn't happen to me.”

Jumping to conclusions: Interpreting the meaning of the situation with little or no evidence.

Mind reading: interpreting the thoughts and beliefs of others without adequate evidence. For example, “She would not go on a date with me. She probably thinks I'm ugly.” Or “I won't even apply for this position because they may not think I'm smart enough.”

Disqualifying the positive: Recognizing only the negative aspects of the situation while ignoring the positive. One might receive many compliments on an evaluation but only focus on a single piece of negative feedback.

All-or-nothing thinking: Thinking absolutes such as “always”, “never”, or “every.” For example, “I never do a good enough job on anything.”

Do you see how this can be problematic? The Bible tells us not to be conformed to the patterns of this world but to be transformed by the renewing of our mind. When you think about it, the pattern of this world relates to the actions and beliefs that human beings have had, in which we use our own reasoning or patterns of thinking absent of faith in God’s word.

While using our own reasoning isn't always bad, it can be flawed. Many of the beliefs that people have are connected to their upbringing, culture, and biases. As a result of people's flawed beliefs, we have seen patterns of genocide, racism, slavery, and many forms of exploitation. Then, as a result of history or our own experiences, we may internalize the associated negative beliefs and look at ourselves or others from that perspective, even if those beliefs do not apply.

"What if the beliefs do apply, Miriam?" I remember hearing about increased scrutiny of African Americans walking around in a store to ensure there was no theft. As an African-American, I internalized this and became very uncomfortable.

I would then project this everywhere I went by thinking that because of my skin color, the employees of the store were uncomfortable with me being there. I then chose to be very methodical and explicit with where I would put items to ensure complete transparency that could diminish any sort of suspicion of my intentions.

I would make my visits very brief. Because of what I heard and how others had been treated, I internalized that information to mean that something was wrong with me. Although there exists a certain, undeniable pattern in this world, I allowed that reality to shape the reflection of how I saw myself. I placed myself in a prison.

Projecting isn't only about race; perhaps you had a bad experience with someone years ago, and you formed a belief that has led to extreme ways of thinking. For example: "They probably don't like me because of what I'm wearing," or "She probably thinks I'm ugly and boring." or "My email had a typo in it, I'll never get the promotion." These misconceptions are projections—errors in our thinking.

Additionally, people's perception of your worth or intrinsic value will naturally vary, especially if their learning is informed by subjectivity (their own perspective), social norms, and not scriptural truths. Now, imagine basing your self-worth on how others perceive you.

Your measure of worth would then vary from person to person depending on each person's viewpoint. As a result, the level of peace that you have in your interactions or environment will also vary, leaving you susceptible to constant instability and insecurity.

When driven by the patterns of this world, it is likely that you might develop belief systems that you then project onto others, resulting in an emotional and mental prison. Conversely, while confined in your prison, you may also be forcing others to be in the prison with you, even though they may not even devalue you the way you devalue yourself.

We often focus on how others see us, but it is imperative for you to correct and let go of negative beliefs that you have about yourself. Remember, as a man thinks in his heart, so is he. What's in your heart? How many opportunities have passed you by as a result of projecting? How many relationships have been damaged or destabilized because of your own insecurity? The wonderful news is, you do not have to live in regret! Your power to change lies with you in the present moment and is prompted by what you choose to consume.

Exercise

Reflect on your relationships at home, outside of your home, and at work. Start identifying the types of thoughts you have projected and how these thoughts have been problematic. Perhaps you've even noticed feelings of anxiety, insecurity, or rage as a result of this type of thinking. With complete honesty, jot down these thoughts. You can refer to the cognitive distortions mentioned earlier and think about how they have shown up in your life.

____

____

____

____

____

____

____

"For there is no partiality with God." (Romans 2:11) This means that He will use any willing vessel for His glory. His use of you will not only result in great things happening but also remind you that your submission to understanding yourself through Him is key.

Visit **https://bonus.pure-ography.com/** to listen to the audio visualization.

Visualization

In this visualization, I want you to envision the Earth. As you see the Earth, I want you to imagine yourself on the outside of it, looking at the planet with God by your side. He begins to tell you about the mission that He has for you. He informs you that the realm of Earth has been corrupted, but your faith in Him will sustain you.

Your faith in who He says you are is the key to being in your purpose and completing your mission. As you take in his word, you hide it in your heart.

Now visualize light entering your heart. He is entrusting you to fulfill your mission and that in itself shows how valuable you are to Him. You now enter into the world again with a new revelation that you didn't have before, which allows you to walk in boldness and freedom.

Your focus is now on fulfilling the purpose in each place that He places you and therefore the peace that you now have is divine because it's not from this world.

Picture yourself no longer projecting, but instead, being peaceful and stable in every place where you previously felt insecure and unstable.

Grab your mirror. It's time for affirmations.

- I am willing to change.
- I'm willing to release criticizing myself.
- I am in this world but I am not of this world.
- I am here on a mission.
- I am choosing to not succumb to the patterns of this world.
- I am choosing to focus on truth.
- I am allowing my mind to be renewed.
- I choose to focus on how God sees me.
- God's thoughts towards me are precious.
- The Holy Spirit leads me into all truth.
- I will know the truth, and the truth will make me free.
- True freedom is found by following the precepts and principles of God.
- I have power love and a sound mind.
- I free myself from the prison that I placed myself in.
- My worth is not determined by people.
- My value is pre-established and does not diminish.
- God's love for me is unconditional.
- I am fearfully and wonderfully made.
- God's plan for me cannot be stopped by any person or pattern in this world.

Chapter 6
Unforgiveness and Offense

"To forgive is to set a prisoner free and discover that the prisoner was you." -Lewis Smedes

Unforgiveness arises from experiencing some form of mistreatment and then harboring the anger and pain caused by that person. The consequence of unforgiveness is becoming a prisoner of the pain that we experienced. No pain you have experienced is worth your purpose. This isn't to diminish or invalidate the pain; instead, it is to emphasize that the pain is not meant to remain with you, just as a wound is not meant to remain open forever.

Many of us have experienced trauma or mistreatment, and instead of letting it go, we have carried it with us as we age. Harboring this resentment and pain can then lead to an emotional infection that inhibits you from living the life that God ordained for you. It can also affect and infect other relationships that you have because the pain that is not transformed is transmitted.

Whatever you allow to reside in your heart is what will manifest in your life. Unforgiveness and perpetuating emotions such as anger, sadness, and fear lead to depression and anxiety.

That's why forgiveness is more beneficial for you than it is for someone else. Unforgiveness can make you dwell on the past, while forgiveness allows you to experience the present and look forward to the future. God calls us to forgive others so He can forgive us as well.

Often, we end up creating an experience of condemnation in our own lives as a result of the contempt we may have towards somebody else. Sometimes we can even be so connected to our experience of pain that it becomes hard to imagine life outside of it. Another result of unforgiveness is being unclear about what our purpose is, especially if we were misused or abused by someone. Let me make it clear: what happened to you does not define your purpose.

Past offenses can attack open-mindedness, leading us to become closed off simply because our brains don't want us to experience that hurt or trauma again, even if it's not a rational fear. Are you ready to let go of the heaviness? Are you ready to create something new?

I remember harboring unforgiveness towards my in-laws for not believing I was compatible with their son. When my spouse would seek marriage advice from them, I would become very defensive and it would only fan the flames. My defensiveness was creating issues with my spouse because of my sensitivity to their initial opinion of me and biases.

I had to let this go, so I could focus on the issue at hand rather than dredging up old troubles, which would lead to a blow-up. My forgiving them had nothing to do with receiving an apology. I had to let go for me, so I could be free.

Moreover, I had to forgive the men who sexually abused me, so I could be whole again. While lack of forgiveness led to anger, disgust, and a low drive for intimacy with my spouse, forgiveness and renewing my mind allowed for restoration and new possibilities that I hadn't previously considered.

It will be difficult to utilize your hands for something new when it is holding something old. You have to let go of the old so that your hands can be free for something new. Offense and trauma lead us to become close-minded. If I'm close-minded, I am not open or truly making myself available to God's desire to restore me and His plan for me.

Last but certainly not least, it is important for you to know that God is a righteous judge. He is THE righteous judge. Nothing goes unnoticed. His word says, "Vengeance is mine." Therefore, trust God that He will vindicate you. David had every right to be offended and have unforgiveness in his heart when his most beloved mentor, King Saul, was chasing after him to kill him. However, I noticed something very peculiar about how David responded.

As hurt as David was, he decided not to speak ill about King Saul and chose not to fight him. He essentially told God, "King Saul is your anointed son. He is your child, Lord, you deal with him." As a result of David doing that, he kept his heart pure, and certainly, God did deal with King Saul.

On multiple occasions, King Saul was delivered into David's hands. While David was in the wilderness, he stumbled upon King Saul sleeping. David could have killed him right there and it would have been over with. This happened other times as well. However, God was showing David that he didn't need to be afraid of King Saul. God had essentially orchestrated that scenario to show him that He is the righteous judge, and He will make your enemies your footstools.

King Saul's envy, hate, and threats were a part of the process of David being positioned to become king later! What you have been through is positioning you for elevation. You may not see how He will elevate you or what that looks like to vindicate you, but just trust that He will address every matter or person that hurt you, and He will elevate you.

Exercise

Reflect on whom you need to forgive. How has unforgiveness affected your life? List them below.

____

____

____

____

____

____

____

____

Visit **https://bonus.pure-ography.com/** to listen to the audio visualization.

Visualization

Imagine you are about to enter a classroom. You see the individuals who mistreated and offended you standing in front of the door. Without overthinking it, you thank each one as you walk forward through the door. You realize that students are inside sitting, and they are waiting for you to take up your post as their teacher. Yes, you are a teacher. You're a great one at that.

You look in your hands, and you suddenly see a book. Looking at the author's name, you see your own name. You are the author. There are stacks of your books that you begin to hand out. Your experiences have enabled you to develop lessons that only you can teach with a high level of mastery. They signed up to take your course because it will help them with their current experiences. They express their gratitude to you for your resilience and for being their teacher.

You leave knowing that none of what you've gone through has been in vain. You leave open to the doors of opportunity that God has in store for you. The following day you find out that your lesson saved someone's life.

Grab your mirror. It's time for affirmations

- I am willing to change.
- I am willing to forgive.
- Forgiveness sets me free.
- I can be restored.
- I am not too much for God to handle.
- God cares for me, so I give Him my burdens.
- I choose to be free.
- My purpose requires my heart's availability, so I give my whole heart to God.
- I release those who have hurt me into God's hands.
- I have learned lessons, and I give myself permission to have healthy boundaries.
- I allow God's love to overtake me.
- I welcome God's peace as I release the pain.
- I have power and love.
- I am stable.
- I am able to rejoice again.
- I am open to love again.
- I am open to what God has in store for me.

Challenge: Pray for someone who hurt you for at least 3 days. Example: "Lord, they are your child. I give them to you to deal with. I trust you will judge them righteously. I release them now."

Whom are you praying for?

(Check off the box below, for each day)

Day 1	
Day 2	
Day 3	

Chapter 7
Shame and Regret

"Where are your accusers?"- Jesus Christ

Are you feeling ashamed about your past? What parts of yourself are you hiding?

The online definition of intimacy is close familiarity or friendship; closeness like the intimacy between a husband and wife, family, or a close friend.

One day, while listening to a teaching, I heard intimacy being broken down as "into me, I see." The inner parts of you that only God and you know about. These are the parts of you that you may show to a select few, and the parts of you that remain hidden or have closed off.

We often lack intimacy in our relationships due to the fear of being vulnerable because of past hurts and disappointments we have experienced. We're often carrying shame and secrets from the past due to the fear of being rejected by those closest to us, whether in the courtship process or in marriage.

In the early stages of dating my spouse, we were in a honeymoon-like stage. Everything seemed fine as long as we stayed above the surface. I was afraid to go deeper because of the pressure I placed on myself to appear a certain way or to maintain a certain image. If he knew certain things about me, would he stay? If he knew my sexual history, would he want to be with me? Accusers often told me that I was a statistic because I had a child, saying no one would want me. These messages haunted me, replaying in my mind over and over.

Not knowing the answers to these questions led me to lie about certain parts of my past because I wasn't sure if he would accept that part of me. However, the Holy Spirit knew these parts quite well; there was no hiding from God. I felt a deep conviction inside me, which led me to be honest, so I told him everything, albeit in stages.

It wasn't pretty. It wasn't easy. There were tears. I was anxious. I sweated. My mascara was all over the place. I didn't know if we could have a future. Nevertheless, within a couple of weeks of being boldly honest, I felt relief. I knew it was less about him accepting me and more about me letting go of the shame I had been carrying. It was about me accepting myself and learning to see myself the way God sees me.

I also remember carrying so much guilt and shame as a result of having an abortion. What would other people think of me? I had another pregnancy following the abortion that ended with a miscarriage. I remember blaming myself, saying, "Miriam, this is your fault. It is because of your actions and you deserve this!" This was harmful. This guilt was causing me grief. I had to give this to God, too, and allow Him to heal me while forgiving myself for the mistakes I'd made.

As long as you are lying to yourself and carrying shame in any part of you due to what you have been through or what you've done, you are not walking in completeness or wholeness. This is dangerous as it will create a barrier to building intimacy later on.

It truly takes faith and courage to decide that parts of you don't have to remain hidden in the past. As mentioned before, if parts of you are still hiding in your past relationships or past hurts, less of you is available for the present or future.

How can you enjoy the now if your attention, or even some of it, is parked in the past? Additionally, I didn't want him to love one part of me or the part of me that appeared to be perfect. I wanted him to choose to love all of me.

He could have left, and that would have been just fine. What was most important was ME loving MYSELF because God loves me unconditionally.

Think about the woman who was about to be stoned. All over, her accusers stood there holding stones, so ready to cast them at her. Jesus drew in the sand and said those without sin cast a stone. None could. He looked at the woman and said, "Where are your accusers?" We often place others on a pedestal, not realizing that they are not perfect either. They have a past. They have sinned. They may not admit it, but the scripture says, "for all have sinned and fall short of the glory of God." (Romans 3:23)

We become afraid, thinking that we have to run away from the words and accusations that people may have for us if they were to know what we've been through, what we've done, and the mistakes we've made. However, as you can see in this example, the permission to be free and love who you are comes with being forgiven by Jesus Christ and accepting His love for you. It doesn't come from a man or woman. It starts with Him and begins with your acceptance of His love for you. Invite God into the intimate places and inward parts of you that you have closed off. If you need help with this, don't hesitate to ask me how.

"And He said to her, 'Daughter, your faith has made you well. Go in peace, and be healed of your affliction." (Mark 5:34)

Therefore, we must strive for wholeness and peace of mind so that we are not plagued by shame, fear, or the past.

Before starting the visualization, take some time to write down some of the negative words and phrases that you remember people saying about you or negative phrases that you have said about yourself.

Example: "I've made too many mistakes. I'm too much for people and no one will love me."

____

____

____

____

Visit **https://bonus.pure-ography.com/** to listen to the audio visualization.

Visualization

For today's visualization, whether you are a man or woman, picture yourself in the same scenario as the woman who was being accused, with a crowd running after her with stones. Instead of her, place your face there. You have been running until you can't run anymore. You have been hiding but can't hide anymore. You've reached a place where you can either get hit by stones or receive salvation. Right in front of you is Jesus Himself.

He begins to speak to you. You also see a crowd behind you. In this crowd are your accusers. Some of them are the faces of various people who have spoken negatively about you. However, you also recognize your face among the crowd. This signifies your own inner criticisms that are compelling you to remain in a cycle of condemnation. They are shouting loudly, voicing all of the things that you wrote above.

As Jesus begins to draw in the sand, the crowd falls silent as He says, "You without sin cast the first stone." Suddenly, you hear the stones drop to the ground. Envision the words falling to the ground like stones. These were the stones that were taking up space in your mind and heart and had even caused your heart to become hard. They begin to walk away, even your own inner critic or critical voice also leaves, and Jesus looks at you asking, "Where are your accusers?". Jesus tells you to go and sin no more as your sins have been forgiven. This is Him also telling you to go and be afraid no more, hide no more, and criticize yourself no more.

You then see yourself walking away, but now you are not alone as He has come into your heart and your mind to heal all of the hidden places. Visualize the light coming into your mind and your heart at the same time. Suddenly, see yourself feeling lighter, bolder, and more courageous because you received His salvation and forgiveness.

Grab your mirror. It's time for Affirmations

- I am not too much for God to handle.
- There is no condemnation for those in Christ Jesus.
- I am forgiven.
- I am loved by the one whose love is perfect.
- I invite God to heal the hidden parts of me today.
- I am invested in changing how I see myself, to align with God's depiction of me.
- I am choosing to embark on a journey of healing and transformation.
- I am willing to change and let go of the shame.
- I am committed to stopping criticizing myself.
- I am receiving divine peace as I say this now.
- I am committed to my transformation.
- I am open to receiving help if I need it.
- I recognize that in the multitude of counselors, there is safety.
- I am not alone.

For the second part of the exercise, write one self-forgiveness statement. For example: "I forgive myself for being emotionally abrasive towards myself and others."

My self-forgiveness statement:

____

____

____

____

____

Now, repeat it seven times. Put a checkmark for each time.

A special note from Coach Miriam

If I'm not mistaken, you are feeling lighter at the end of this. This is the beginning of a transformative process where the hardened parts of your heart will become softened and open up to receive love because you are receiving God's love. Stay committed to seeing yourself the way God sees you.

Chapter 8
Perfectionism and Performance

"He knew about every mistake you would make, and still chose you."

The American Psychological Association defines perfectionism as the tendency to demand of others or of oneself an extremely high or even flawless level of performance, in excess of what is required by the situation.

Often, perfectionism, along with emphasis on performance is driven by the need to maintain one's reputation, despite the unrealistic and excessive pressure that one may place on oneself unnecessarily. Perfectionism leaves no room for flexibility, mercy, or grace—all of which are vital in every aspect of our lives. In my counseling work, I've encountered people from all walks of life—athletic college superstars with full-ride scholarships from major organizations, leaders in high positions, and everyone in between.

Some, due to perfectionism, have become burdened and lost their zeal for the very thing they once cherished. Others are apprehensive about going for new positions or trying something new, because of the fear of making mistakes or being a disappointment to others. Some have also wrapped their self-esteem within their performance, and then feel bad about themselves if they have an off day.

Instead of finding enjoyment in the mission and allowing oneself to learn through mistakes, many have become miserable because they focus solely on how they are evaluated by others especially themselves. Remember, “to err is human,” which is why God is so rich in mercy and grace. His word says this: "But God demonstrates His own love toward us, in that while we were still sinners, Christ died for us." (Romans 5:8)

We didn't have to do anything to earn His love, and when He is looking at you it's like He is looking at Himself because you are made in His image. His love for you is unconditional, and nothing can separate you from His love. He knew about every mistake you would make and still chose you. Within those mistakes are lessons that you have learned that help you to become a better person when you implement them.

Therefore, we must alter our perception of mistakes, ensuring we do not condemn ourselves or be overly critical. Condemnation can actually keep you in a cycle of apprehension and/or sadness.

A healthier approach is to be compassionately constructive with ourselves in a way that continues to build us up and encourages us to move forward without the pressure to be perfect. It's about acknowledging that we all fall down but get back up again.

Unfortunately, we have forgotten how to encourage ourselves as we live in a judgmental and critical society that begins at a very young age.

When learning to walk as a toddler, perfection was neither expected nor required, and falling down was part of the process. Whenever you would fall, encouraging people around told you to get back up. When children are encouraged in this way, they become aware that falling is a part of learning to stand. They may be careful while learning to walk as a result of falling. Such compassionate guidance instills courage and fosters progress.

There are few professions that actually require perfectionism. Surgeons, for instance, require precision and accuracy. And let me tell you, even they have liability insurance to cover potential mistakes. The only perfect person is Jesus, and yet, they still crucified him. Yes, He gave Himself up to be crucified. I'm sure you get my point. It is better to have a spirit of Excellence rather than Perfectionism while making room for God's grace and mercy. Show yourself love because God loves you.

Embrace a spirit of excellence that accommodates practice, mistakes, correction compassion, and growth!

Exercise

How has perfectionism impacted your life?

____

____

____

____

Visit **https://bonus.pure-ography.com/** to listen to the audio visualization.

Visualization

Imagine yourself in a maze. You have been stuck in one corner and it has created delay and emotional depletion. At the end of the maze lies the finish line. You had previously imposed the idea that you had to reach the finish line within a certain time frame because of how others may see you and what they may say if you don't finish it by then. However, these pressures were self-imposed.

As a result of all this pressure built up, you recognize that you're putting off doing what you have set your mind to do, which is finishing at your own pace.

You then take seven deep breaths. With each deep breath, you release the pressure to get to the finish line in a certain way and timeframe. With each inhale, you breathe in peace, understanding that it's okay to make wrong turns; you can always turn around and find a new path. The peace you inhale fills you up in the place of the pressure that is now gone.

As you navigate the maze, you make a few wrong turns but no longer emotionally berate yourself. You take note of the turns and go a different way. You keep going until you reach the end. You're proud of yourself for not giving up and for following through regardless of the pivots or pauses that you made along the way. You did it!

Grab your mirror. It's time for affirmations

- I relinquish the pressure to perform.
- I am embracing my authentic self in Christ Jesus.
- In God, I live, move, and have my being.
- Everything that I need to know comes to me because of the Holy Spirit within me.
- I welcome grace today and relinquish guilt and grief.
- I am made in God's image.
- I am fearfully and wonderfully made.
- I can do all things through Christ who gives me strength.
- Even if I mess up today, I can try again tomorrow.
- Every mistake I make is a lesson learned.
- There is someone who will benefit from my experiences.
- Even if I fall down, I can rise again.
- My past is my push for my purpose.
- I am teachable and capable of learning.
- I am here to learn and grow.

Scripture: “A righteous man Falls seven times and gets back up. Proverbs 24:16”

Challenge: If you make a mistake this week, instead of responding with criticism, respond with compassion. Tell yourself, “It’s okay, I can try again or find a new way!”

Chapter 9
Void and Lust

"Delight yourself in the Lord and He will give you the desires of your heart." Psalms 37:4

Some of my clients have discussed how their addiction to alcohol, pornography, and casual hookups initially began with just wanting companionship. After failed relationships, along with contending with themselves about maintaining the responsibilities of adulthood, they began to feel bad about themselves and search for quick fixes.

I've observed how what starts off as a genuine desire for love can turn into lust if we misunderstand our purpose, lack maturity, and fail to understand our value. Failure to understand your true value indicates that there are voids that you may have, potentially manifesting as feelings of emptiness or even loneliness. There may also be some fears of abandonment and rejection which may lead to a lack of commitment and lower standards.

However, for those who do desire marriage, you are not meant to be alone. This is also different from loneliness. Even in Genesis, God made Adam and said it was not good for him to be alone. He wasn't designed to be by himself and therefore God made Eve. Eve was not an afterthought. She had a purpose. She was beautiful and brilliant. Their purpose was to commune with God, love each other, serve, and dominate. Before Adam came to know Eve, God had given him an assignment—he was a cultivator in the garden. He was established.

Every individual needs to understand their assignment(s) as there is a need within each person to cultivate something and make an impact. It is also important to be established and financially secure before engaging in dating or beginning the process of courtship. When we look at Eve, she is most noticeably known for being deceived. In search for love, I've seen many women forget to associate God as the ultimate source of love. God is the way, the TRUTH, and the life. This means that His way leads to freedom and abundant life!

Not understanding God's love for you can impact how you see yourself and your value. As a result, instead of navigating by means of partnering with God, they put themselves in situations that end in deception and disappointment. This is often because their low self-esteem leads them to settle for low-standard partnerships. As a result, we may end up making a man our assignment instead of being led to one who already has and understands his assignment, and vice versa.

Two different outcomes can result from being led to an individual who understands their assignment versus one who doesn't understand their assignment or purpose. The difference is aimlessness, which is often connected to voids that the individual is experiencing as a result of not understanding their calling or purpose. That is not something you can fill, no matter how hard you try.

If someone doesn't understand their mission and their purpose, aimlessness is inevitable because they're not moving toward the direction where their destiny lies. The lack of understanding of one's purpose can stem from brokenness, leading men and women to seek temporary satisfaction and pleasure, such as through pornography. masturbation, casual hookups, drugs, alcohol, gambling, gluttony, excessive gaming, etc.

They call this "just going with the flow," but that is because there's no sense of direction.

Dating can often be challenging when values are compromised. Here are some of the other nuances that I have picked up or thoughts you may experience while dating:

- "By the second or third date, he seems to want to take things further."
- "I'm trying to be nice because that is a part of my personality; however, it seems like he is interpreting those signals as me wanting to be physical."
- "I just want to enjoy the date, without being touched or kissed without my consent." "My gut is telling me that I don't want to go on another date, but what if I'm cutting off 'the one'?"
- "I'm afraid of being too judgmental, to the point I miss out on an opportunity." "I'm feeling friend

vibes with him, but I don't want to hurt his feelings."

- "It seems that I have to be physical if I want to date." Note that men too can feel these pressures as well.

Yeah, I have been there. I remember forcing myself to go to prom with someone that I neither liked nor felt attracted to. I just wanted to be nice. I remember him telling me, "I just want to kiss you." I remember thinking to myself, "Why in the world would you think I would let you?" I certainly did not give off the notion that I was interested in any type of physical advancement. We did not text prior to him asking me to prom. We did not talk on the phone. We did not hang out at school. Nor did we do any of these things after. In this instance, I realized the importance of not just "going with the flow." Regardless of your reasons, the flow can lead you anywhere and potentially to a destination you don't want to be.

"Going with the flow" can lead to you being touched in a way that you don't want to be touched. The flow can lead to intimacy in a way that you never intended. The flow could lead to a hookup that leaves spiritual hooks in you, forming what some might call a soul tie. The flow could lead to emotional damage.

It is crucial to have boundaries, as they keep you headed in a direction conducive to a healthy relationship and establishment. If your goal is to settle down with the right person, discretion and discernment early on is important.

So, why do we sometimes lack discretion and discernment, opting to just "go with the flow" and end up perpetuating cycles of void and lust?

Often, this is due to unresolved past traumas or wounds, as mentioned before. We might then jump from one relationship to the next, assuming that it will provide the solution. However, instead of moving towards healthiness, we're just hurt people moving—moving away from one bad situation, to another version of it.

These are the questions I would ask you:

- Are there past relationships that you have not gotten over yet?
- Are you struggling with your self-worth?
- Do you fear setting boundaries or saying no?
- Do you feel that maintaining a relationship even though you have seen red flags is better than being lonely? Are you feeling up any voids with temporary pleasures as mentioned above, which can actually lead to significant problems?

If you've answered yes to any of these questions, I would say that you are not ready for dating BUT you are ready for development. And as you develop and grow, so will your self-esteem, discernment, and discretion.

"Delight yourself also in the Lord, And He shall give you the desires of your heart." (Psalms 37). When you delight yourself in Him, it's a process of Him developing you for that desire. If you had the desire before you were ready, that desire can become detrimental to your emotional and spiritual well-being. God is love and the ultimate source of it.

As you get to know Him, you get to know His love for you, which helps you heal and change your self-perception. Delighting in Him is a process of you becoming full of His essence. It is the manifestation of His DNA within you, a process where we Dive into God, Neutralize those negative beliefs, and Activate power and purpose.

As a result, there is a new standard because He has truly satisfied the hunger and thirst in your soul, something no one else can actually fulfill. Why can no one else fulfill it? Because He is the standard.

Then, this standard in you becomes your selector. Have you ever heard those sayings like "real recognizes real," "the spirit bears witness with another spirit," and "the deep calleth unto the deep"? As a result of your growth, the standard that you will have for yourself will help you select your future spouse versus settling for temporary satisfaction.

Signs that you're ready:

- You know your value.
- You know your purpose and assignment.
- You're not afraid to say no.
- You're not afraid to establish boundaries.

- You're okay with parting ways with someone who doesn't have the same values as you do.
- You're not operating from a scarcity mindset, because you understand that if you have the desire, God has designed it, and the right person is there for you.
- You are patient, purposeful, and financially stable.

Coach Miriam's words of wisdom:

1. Being nice isn't just about saying yes. It also includes assertiveness, boundaries, and saying no.

2. Understand that you are not responsible for how somebody perceives themselves. (Proverbs 23:7)

3. Know your worth, value, and assignment.

4. Your no doesn't diminish anyone's value.

5. Understand that seeing other people disappointed is something we grew up trying to avoid. Many of us were taught and groomed to focus on pleasing others through our behavior, getting good grades, and so forth. In this case, give yourself permission to be uncomfortable even if they are disappointed with your no or with your boundaries because their disappointment in response to your no did not come from a bad place.

   6. Seek professional help to ensure you've healed from any past traumas or hurts.

Exercise

What have you learned about yourself after reading this chapter, and what are some behaviors you'd like to change?

____

____

____

____

____

____

____

____

Visit **https://bonus.pure-ography.com/** to listen to the audio visualization.

Visualization

In this visualization, I want you to picture yourself in your bedroom. You're sitting on your bed, and while sitting there, you begin to pray. As you pray for direction in the area of dating and marriage, you begin to experience a deeper understanding of God's love for you.

You also begin to feel His peace and divine strength, visualized in the form of a bright light, entering your heart.

This peace and strength will help you be patient and begin any process needed to help you with healing, including partnering with professional help. Picture yourself spending time with God and enjoying this intimate relationship with Him. Notice that you no longer engage in unhealthy habits, as you have now formed healthier ones.

Visualize yourself engaging in these healthy habits. Finally, imagine time has passed. Look at yourself in the mirror. From within, you're emotionally healed and whole. Outwardly, you look amazing. See yourself smiling. You are now ready for your next chapter.

Grab your mirror: It's time for affirmations.

- I am fearfully and wonderfully made.
- I have learned from my past experiences, and I'm ready to implement those lessons.
- I am operating with discernment.
- Today, I welcome godly wisdom to help me navigate.
- I'm at peace because I know God is with me.
- I Look to God as my ultimate source of love.
- I am patient while He is developing me.
- I choose to delight myself in the Lord and He will give me the desires of my heart.
- My faith has made me whole.
- I am moving patiently because I know my needs are met.

- God has a plan and a purpose for me.
- I have a God-ordained spouse.
- I am blessed with a kingdom marriage.
- I am blessed with a God-fearing marriage.
- My steps are ordered by the Lord.
- God leads me down the path of righteousness.

Chapter 10
Ungodly Soul Ties

"Either you've accepted somebody else's identity, or you know who you are in Christ."

You might be wondering what "soul ties" are, and how they are relevant to mind purification. Soul ties basically mean being spiritually linked to someone in a way that can be positive or negative as a result of your interaction or connection with them. The interesting thing is that soul ties can also impact one's mind, and I'll tell you how to break them below.

Ways to know if you have ungodly soul ties

- You haven't gotten over an ex
- You find yourself fixated on someone with whom you no longer have a connection.
- You experience inappropriate thoughts or imagery about someone you were or are connected to.
- You often recall sexual encounters or conversations with individuals from the past
- You've experienced sexual trauma
- You are in co-dependent relationships (this could even be with parents or friends)
- You still hold items from an ex (in addition to the above)

(If you identify with any of the above, sever those ties today with the prayer at the end of this chapter.)

Even though the concept of soul ties is not explicitly mentioned in the Bible, the scripture does talk about souls being knitted together.

An example of a healthy soul tie was between two friends in the Bible: Jonathan and David. "Now when he had finished speaking to Saul, the soul of Jonathan was knit to the soul of David, and Jonathan loved him as his own soul." (1 Samuel 18:1)

An example of an unhealthy attachment or soul tie is illustrated in the relationship between Jacob and Benjamin. The scripture says, "Now therefore, when I come to your servant my father, and the lad is not with us, since his life is bound up in the lad's life, it will happen, when he sees that the lad is not with us, that he will die."(Genesis 44:30)"."

This verse is about when Joseph's brothers went to Egypt for food during a famine. They did not recognize him as their brother. They had sold him into slavery due to jealousy and envy. It had been years since they'd seen each other. Joseph was giving them orders but had not disclosed his real identity. Jacob, Joseph's father, did not know Joseph was alive as the brothers had faked his death.

As a result, Jacob developed an unhealthy attachment to Benjamin, who was Joseph's biological brother and the last son of his now-deceased wife Rachel.

Therefore, if Jacob had been protective before, his protectiveness escalated to the point of dependency. He became so attached to Benjamin that his sons sincerely believed that their father would die if anything happened to Benjamin.

Without a doubt, Jacob went through a lot, especially what his sons put him through. Grieving is natural; however, in his grieving process, he ended up keeping one child extremely close, probably to the point of dictating Benjamin's every move and controlling his life. That is unhealthy.

Some individuals may have unhealthy soul ties with their parents, where they are unsure of how to distinguish between honor and obedience as adults. They may even question their own ability to make decisions and follow the voice of God, primarily because the voices of their parents are so amplified in their heads. This can be the case, no matter how old one becomes, especially if they were constantly criticized and are co-dependent with that parent or authoritative figure.

Such unhealthy attachments could also manifest as a hurdle in the marriage, preventing the two from cleaving to each other due to their unhealthy relationships with their parents.

There are those who have unhealthy soul ties with friends, where they may prioritize the friendship and the needs of that friend over their own needs, without reciprocity. This excessive loyalty, lacking balance, is unhealthy.

Other individuals may also have unhealthy soul ties with ex-partners. Despite no longer being in the relationship, they may find themselves still thinking of them in an unhealthy way. Perhaps they had sexual encounters when in that relationship. This can foster deeper soul ties. Red flags for such an unhealthy tie may include being haunted by your past, obsessing about an ex, missing that ex, constantly checking those ex's social media accounts, and more. This is unhealthy and not conducive to forging a healthy attachment in your marriage or future marriage.

These ungodly soul ties need to be severed and broken! It's time to remove the hooks that could be dragging you and keeping you from where God wants you to be in your marriage, future marriage, or any aspect of your life.

The good news is that God is in the business of restoring your soul. You can begin by removing items that you received from an ex or anyone you've had an unhealthy relationship with. Ask God to reveal this to you —be it pictures, jewelry, clothes, etc.

Say this prayer:

I renounce any ungodly soul ties that I may have formed with anyone in the past, including past friendships, exes, and authority figures (such as leaders or parents) (Name each person.) I repent of idolizing any relationship and putting it on a pedestal where you, Lord, should be. I forgive anyone who has hurt me, and I forgive myself for having hurt anyone.

Lord, I beseech you to sever any ungodly tie or attachment that I have with anyone that has resulted in my fixation on them or idolization of them. Please sever any ungodly soul tie that Has resulted in me being manipulated or manipulating others. Please sever any soul ties that have led me towards fear of abandonment or rejection.

Please sever any ungodly tie that is unknown, and bring to my remembrance anything else that I need to repent of and renounce in Jesus' name, amen.

Congratulations, the soul tie is severed. Remember, your healing journey is a process, and this is just the beginning. Don't hesitate to reach out if you need support in the form of coaching.

"Either you've accepted somebody else's Identity, or you've come to know who you are in Christ." It's time for you to know who you are in Christ now that the hooks have been removed!

Visit **https://bonus.pure-ography.com/** to listen to the audio visualization.

Visualization

In this visualization, picture yourself and those whom you had an unhealthy soul tie with. It could be a parent, an ex, a church leader, a family member, or a friend. Picture yourself initially tied to them and then picture the tie being cut with huge scissors. After the tie has been severed, picture God stepping in to hold your hand. As He holds your hand, see His light coming into your heart.

This is His love restoring every fragmented piece of you. He tells you to trust the process of knowing who you are in Him. You suddenly realize that you no longer have to keep looking back at the past or for the approval of those that you had an unhealthy relationship or a tie with. You start moving forward because God is on your side.

Grab your mirror. It's time for affirmations

- I am no longer stuck in the past. The best is yet to come.
- God has great plans for my life.
- I am more committed to who I am becoming in Christ.
- My focus is on God and not on anyone else.
- I forgive everyone and maintain healthy boundaries for myself.
- I am tied to God.
- The Lord is my stronghold and my portion.
- I am no longer double-minded but am spiritually minded.
- I have life and peace because I am led by the Spirit and not my flesh.
- I am healed and whole.

- Greater is He who is in me than he who is in the world.
- Every addictive cycle in my life is broken.
- I redirect my thoughts to things that are lovely and virtuous.
- I am pure.
- I am restored.
- I am redeemed.
- I am loved by the One whose love is perfect.

Chapter 11
Sadness

"Many times, we need someone to wake us up and speak truth into emotionally desolate places that we have normalized. Truth yields freedom!"

Before I begin working with some clients, they often report a general feeling of sadness. Sometimes they can't pinpoint the root of the sadness; they just know that there is something missing. For some, this may evolve into apathy or not caring. But even underneath the apathy lies emotional depletion because of a constant mental battle to be happy. Every day can feel like it takes a concerted effort to get up and do the day-to-day tasks.

Sometimes, there's even isolation and a tendency to isolate oneself. As I have highlighted throughout this book, your feelings and behaviors are connected to the beliefs you have. The beliefs you have come from some experience that you have had and/or grief, such as the loss of a loved one, and not knowing how to move forward.

Regardless of the time passed since the event, one might remain emotionally anchored to the point of the loss. Sadness can also result from needs that aren't being addressed or met. Some clients even report grieving the loss of childhood due to being emotionally neglected during those years.

Sadness is essentially an emptiness that a person is experiencing which is equivalent to having a hole in the heart. The heart is needed to pump blood to other organs; however, it cannot be as effective in sustaining the other organs if it is unhealthy.

The story of the Samaritan woman who met Jesus at the well is an excellent example. She was a woman who was sad and eventually settled. Do you feel like you're settling or just surviving?

This story takes place at a well. A well is a deep hole in the ground where water is drawn. The woman came to the well because she was literally thirsty, but Jesus saw that there was a spiritual thirst and an emotional need. "Jesus said, 'If you knew the gift of God, and who it is who says to you, "Give Me a drink," you would have asked Him, and He would have given you living water.'" (John 4:10) (He was referring to something spiritual). She didn't think He could help her until He revealed secrets about her life.

"Jesus said to her, 'Go call your husband and come back.' The woman answered and said, 'I have no husband. Jesus said to her, 'You are right in saying you have no husband, for you have had FIVE husbands, and the one you now have is not your husband!'" (John 4:16-18) Suddenly, she was shocked, then received His salvation. Truly, many times we need someone to awaken us and speak truth into emotionally desolate places that we have normalized. Truth yields freedom!

The Samaritan woman experienced disappointment, sadness, and challenges in relationships. FIVE marriages and FIVE divorces led her to settle for a non-marital living situation with her partner. Sometimes we think that the antidote to sadness is companionship.

While companionship is not a bad thing, starting a relationship for the purpose of filling an emotional void will not work. This can lead to a codependent relationship, or place a burden on the individual that you are connecting to while seeking to find peace or happiness. This can eventually lead to burnout. In her pursuit for the perfect person or companion, she was an individual who was hurting and in need of help. There was something profound that she was lacking until she met Jesus.

The remedy for sadness lies in embracing God's love, seeking professional help, and taking action.

Exercise

Look at each category and write down the issues or challenges you're facing in each area. Be honest with yourself as awareness is key.

Spiritual

____

____

____

____

____

Self

Relationships

Health/Wellness

Finances

Career/ Calling

Note down what can help you make the necessary changes: Some of these things may involve investments, but remember that good Investments yield great returns. Examples include coaching, counseling, discovery of interest, accountability, personal trainer, nutritionist, learning/webinar, communication skills, etc.

Add steps and timeframes: For instance, "I will contact a counselor or coach by Tuesday of this week," "I will write down my discovery list by Friday of this week." Be realistic and intentional with these time frames. Clients who have the most success are those who put it on their calendars and follow through!

____

____

____

____

____

____

____

Visit **https://bonus.pure-ography.com/** to listen to the audio visualization.

Visualization

Visualize yourself in your room. It's morning, and you're awake. You've completed your morning routine and fixed your bed. You decide to take a walk in a nearby park because you know exercise helps to boost your mood. It's a sunny day with clear skies. Now, imagine yourself walking in the park. You notice a smile on your face, which is one of your favorite features about yourself.

As you walk, you come across a note with your name on it. You pick it up, and it says, "You will have a prosperous and bright future," signed by God, your Father. Suddenly, you feel the warmth of the sunlight on your skin. You begin to feel hopeful again, along with immense gratitude that you're alive. Take a deep breath.

Remember to follow through with the steps that you identified earlier.

Grab your mirror. It's time for affirmations

- God woke me up today for a purpose.
- I am loved by God.
- God wants me to live.
- I choose to live.
- An abundant life is my portion.
- I'm committed to becoming the truest version of myself, which is in Christ.
- God has great plans for my life.
- Freedom is my portion.
- God's grace is sufficient for me.
- When I am weak, He makes me strong.
- I allow myself to depend on God's strength.
- I am willing to stop criticizing myself.
- I am willing to change.
- Peace is my portion.
- I am motivated, and I have hope.
- My future is bright!

Chapter 12
Intrusive Thoughts

"It is time for you to become the director and driver of your thoughts."

"My mind is spiraling." "I can't seem to control my thoughts." "The craziest thoughts just appear out of nowhere." Have you ever used any of these phrases? I know I have. I would constantly find myself in the same cycle of heaviness because of intrusive thoughts. According to an article written by Nebraska Medicine Behavioral Health, "Intrusive thoughts are unwanted thoughts, images, impulses, or urges that can occur spontaneously or be triggered by something. It might be violent or sexual, or a recurring fear that you'll do something inappropriate or embarrassing. Whatever the content, it's often unsettling and may bring on feelings of worry or shame. The more you try to push the thought from your mind, the more it persists."

Many clients I've worked with have expressed challenges with trying to stop these intrusive thoughts and found them distressing. As I've mentioned before, these thoughts often develop from a traumatic event or significant challenge that has circulated in your mind time and time again. This is also referred to as cognitive rehearsal, similar to how you would rehearse for a theatrical play.

Think about the numerous hours that go into practicing lines and repeating those lines, regardless of whether you say them in front of the mirror or recite them with a co-actor. The goal is to memorize it for the presentation and so you keep repeating and saying the lines. In this case, you want it to take up capacity within your mind so that you can recall everything that you have rehearsed for the appointed time. This process demands intention, consistency, and discipline. It doesn't just happen.

However, the reverse is also true. Often, when we experience something traumatic, we have a tendency to rehearse that event as a defense mechanism. Our mind wants us to remember to help keep us alert and prepared. These cognitive rehearsals or intrusive thoughts are an overcorrection to the mind's way of trying to alert you. It goes into overdrive, thinking of every worst-case scenario. While the brain's focus is on safety, if the irrational thoughts are not redirected, this can lead to an obsession or fixation.

My mind would even fabricate images of people and scenarios. This turned out to be very problematic for me and stole my peace of mind until I learned how to become the director of my thoughts.

You might be experiencing intrusive thoughts as a result of sexual trauma, physical trauma, emotional trauma, or even due to the traumatic loss of a loved one, or a child. Even receiving unexpected horrific news can be traumatizing. These events cause us to look at life completely differently. While some individuals gain a new lease on life and actually feel free, others may become trapped due to the heaviness associated with this form of mental weight. This mental weight makes it difficult to move forward, essentially making you feel trapped and stagnant within the same cycle.

Unable to break this thinking or living pattern, some people become discouraged and seek solace in temporary comfort. That's when they may begin developing unhealthy coping mechanisms that provide superficial, fleeting relief but don't address the underlying issue.

Some clients that I've spoken to about this were just trying to escape the mental anguish. Their unhealthy coping mechanisms included alcoholism, hookups, substance abuse, pornography, or masturbation. Concerning pornography, many feel guilty for engaging in it and actually do not want to continue this behavior but find it hard to stop. In essence, one unhealthy fixation is temporarily replaced by another unhealthy compulsion or obsession. Pornography, just like substance abuse, can have detrimental effects on the mind.

These unhealthy coping mechanisms may provide temporary pleasure but end up worsening the issue. Unhealthy coping mechanisms do not address the root of the problem, merely scratching the surface of the issue that is, in fact, buried deep within.

Earlier, I mentioned that it is time for you to become the director and driver of your thoughts. Thoughts will constantly come, but Philippians 4: 8 advises us to think about things that are pure, lovely, and of good report. Again, this reminds us that we have to be intentional about what we think about, and that is how we become the director of the show versus an actor who is just rehearsing or wandering. You are called to direct. Regardless of how long you've been stuck in this mental pattern, you can begin making changes today!

Exercise: *Negative Thought Prison*

Grab a fresh piece of paper, and write “Negative Thought Prison” at the top. You don’t belong confined behind those bars or in the mental bondage that you’ve been in. Those thoughts do. It’s time to place them there.

On this paper, list down all the intrusive thoughts that have been weighing you down. You can be as detailed as you want. A few examples can be:

- “I wish I could just disappear.”

- “I’ll always be alone.”
- “I’m not smart enough.”
- “I’ll always be poor.”
- “Life is too hard.”
- “I’m going to be assaulted,”
- “I think about hurting someone because I was hurt,”
- “I think about causing physical harm to myself or others,”
- “No one will love me,”

- "I think about becoming sick or family members becoming sick or dying.
"

After you are done, crumple the paper up and toss it in the trash, while saying from the depth of your heart, "I remove you."

Below, note how you feel after completing this exercise.

____

____

____

____

____

Visit **https://bonus.pure-ography.com/** to listen to the audio visualization.

Visualization

In this visualization, I want you to imagine yourself standing outside on a path. This is the path where your purpose lies, but intrusive thoughts have hindered your steady progress. Visualize yourself praying, asking God to give you power love, and a sound mind. He fulfills your request.

Now picture a beam of light descending from heaven, and shining upon your head. You suddenly know what you need to do. Visualize yourself removing the thoughts, as if you are removing something old from the refrigerator that needs to be tossed out.

Each time you reach in, you're grabbing an old intrusive thought that you've realized is actually powerless. Picture yourself placing the thoughts in this trash can. Identify each thought that needs to be placed in that trash can, and then from your heart say, “I cast you down and remove you. You don’t align with what God says about me. I trust His word and plan for my life.”

Do this until you have removed all of the thoughts. Now envision yourself smiling because you are free, confidently moving down your path of purpose with confidence.

Grab your mirror. It's time for affirmations (It’s not enough to remove those thoughts. They need to be replaced).

- I am releasing the mental weights.
- I am pure.
- I am a worthy child of God.
- I am the righteousness of God.
- I am spiritually minded and I receive life and peace.
- I am committed to understanding my purpose in God.
- I am forgiven.
- God gives me a pure heart.
- I am more than a conqueror.
- I am not those negative thoughts.

- I am who God says I am.
- God wants me to live.
- I receive mercy and grace every day.
- I receive peace today.
- I forgive others.
- My impact is undeniable.
- There is a calling on my life.
- Others will be blessed by my testimony.
- My healed wounds will become somebody's wings.

Additional Exercise: Formulate new thoughts in accordance with Philippians 4:8. Have fun with this!

What is a truthful thought you can think of?

____

____

____

What is an honorable thought you can think of?

____

____

____

What is a pure thought you can think of?

____

____

____

What is a lovely thought you can think of?

___

___

___

What's a thought that involves a good report?

___

___

___

Now be intentional about setting your mind on what you've written!

Chapter 13
Easily Distracted and Procrastination

"It's time to become acquainted with the focused and proactive version of yourself."

According to the American Psychological Association, a researcher stated that the average attention span has dwindled down to about 40 seconds within the past five to six years, particularly in the context of multi-tasking and stress. They discovered a correlation between the frequency of attention-switching and stress.

Many of my clients have reported struggling with maintaining focus and being easily distracted. They have created long to-do lists, leading them to feel stressed out about having to complete all the tasks. Some resort to multitasking, but then it creates room for error and compromises the quality of their work.

Some people even report the difficulty of "adulting" (the process of taking ownership of decision-making and completing responsibilities), no matter how much they are aging. Some feel like they are missing out on the enjoyment of life because of tasks they are obligated to do. They may then add some type of entertaining element such as social media, podcasts, or television, to the mix;

however, this ends up dividing their attention and slowing down their progress. Or, they may not engage in the "responsible" task at all. Whether this be work-related, health-related, or household-related.

I have noticed that mental wandering can also come in conjunction with being easily distracted. You might ask, "What is mental wandering, Miriam?" I am glad you asked! I remember looking into thin air, utterly lost in thought. When asked what I was daydreaming about, I'd say, "I don't know. I was just thinking." I would allow my mind to wander and think of anything aside from the traumas and hardships that I had gone through.

What I had gone through had become a normal phenomenon to rehearse, as I discussed in the previous chapter. However, the way that I would combat it at times was by allowing my mind to wander. Sometimes I'd take myself into some sort of fantasy land where everything was cozy and comfortable. I had fun there. I'd see myself laughing. Everything seemed to be easy and allowed me to mentally escape.

As long as I was on a mental vacation, the negative feelings would also subside. This is when I began to notice the connection between my thoughts and my feelings. This wasn't bad in itself. However, it didn't directly address the issue. Our brains have neural pathways, which are essentially the habits we create that make us inclined to do something over and over again. In one way or another, you are strengthening your neural pathways.

I began to strengthen the neural pathways that made mental wandering a familiar thing to do. This was a form of escapism, which in turn, amplified my susceptibility to being continuously distracted.

I would put off projects and tasks. This phenomenon is partly due to not trusting oneself or having a lot of doubt in oneself, leading to fear, which ultimately leads to procrastination. Moreover, my mind had worked out so much in fantasyland or had been consumed by fear and avoidance that I didn't want to put forth the mental energy for the task that I needed to do.

Have you ever found yourself just mindlessly scrolling on social media because it seemed easier to do than completing a task? I know I have. It's time to become acquainted with the focused and proactive version of yourself.

Exercise

How has being easily distracted or procrastination impacted your life?

____

____

____

____

____

____

Let's discuss three strategies that can help overcome being easily distracted and procrastinating.

1. The "Do it now" Strategy

Years ago, I read a fictional book containing effective strategies for completing tasks as soon as possible. The protagonist was struggling with getting anything done. He was overwhelmed with all the responsibilities of being a realtor. He didn't feel like calling clients. He didn't feel like following up on leads (prospective clients) or creating marketing ads. He constantly compared himself to others and felt like he should be further along. This only made him feel worse. He was even struggling with doing his laundry and maintaining good health, including brushing his teeth regularly. Even though this book is fictional, this story resonates with many adults.

He attended a conference where he learned about being intentional about following through with one's tasks and ideas. The longer one deliberates on it with no action, the more one tends to postpone. They bought red bands that they put around their wrists to remind them to act immediately. They would snap the band and say, "Do it now."

They were doing this neuro-linguistic exercise in which they were retraining their brains that it was in them to get it done, and they didn't have to overthink it. Sometimes we are just in analysis paralysis, overthinking every step.

I'm not saying we should not be prepared, but sometimes we simply overthink and this can be draining. I recommend that you get a red band and put it around your wrist at the beginning of your day.

This is something you can keep on your bedside. You put it on, and as you are about to do a task, or when you have an idea, snap the wrist and say, “Do it now.” Then follow it with an action. I have tried this, and it was effective! In no time, you will begin to see changes.

2. The “3 Things” Strategy

Make a to-do list of what you need to do before moving on.

There have been instances with both my clients and myself where we overloaded our to-do lists. Consequently, we’d end up feeling stressed because of the number of tasks that we needed to do. With this strategy, you only pick three tasks off the list that need completion Ensure that at least one of those three things is something that you have been putting off. When you finish the three things, you are telling your brain that you can do it and you are giving it new information that you are trustworthy to follow through with being a responsible person and an adult.

If you choose to employ this technique, what are the three things you need to do today?

___

___

___

___

3. The Pomodoro Technique

The Pomodoro Technique essentially trains people to focus on tasks better by limiting the length of time they attempt to maintain that focus and ensuring recuperative breaks. The method also helps them overcome their tendencies to procrastinate or multitask, both of which are known to impair productivity.

The Pomodoro Technique is a time management method based on 25-minute stretches of focused work broken by five-minute breaks. Longer breaks, typically 15 to 30 minutes, are taken after four consecutive work intervals. Each work interval is called a Pomodoro, the Italian word for tomato (plural: Pomodoro).

The Core Process serves as the foundation for achieving the Pomodoro Technique in a sustainable way. It defines the following five steps for staying focused on the tasks at hand throughout the day:

1. Choose a task for the current Pomodoro.
2. Set the timer to 25 minutes.
3. Work on the task until the timer sounds, then record the completion of the Pomodoro.
4. Take a short break (5 minutes)
5. After four Pomodoro, take a longer break

Visit **https://bonus.pure-ography.com/** to listen to the audio visualization.

Visualization

In this visualization, I'd like you to picture yourself in a place that is most conducive for you to achieve mental focus and sharpness. For some, this may be a library or a coffee shop. You decided to go there because you are now intentional about setting yourself up for success. Visualize yourself well-prepared to utilize one of the above techniques.

You have realized that you are completely empowered to do everything that you set your mind to. All you had to do was begin. Envision yourself doing each task and completing it. With each task that you complete, you tell yourself 'Good job,' and to keep on going. You're not overwhelmed, as you are proactive with starting and completing the tasks. See yourself smiling.

Grab your mirror. It's time for affirmations

- I am willing to change.
- I'm willing to try new techniques.
- I am becoming patient more and more each day.
- I am choosing to encourage myself.
- I take care of myself so I can take care of others.
- Winning is in my DNA.
- I was designed for success.

- I am more committed to who I am in Christ than the past version of me.
- I am productive.
- I choose to focus on truth.
- God gives me strength.
- In truth, I have freedom.
- Limitations have broken off of me today.
- My focus is sharp.
- I am mentally sharp.
- I complete the tasks I begin.
- I choose not to compare myself to others because I honor the journey that I am in.
- I am reaching every destination that I set my mind to.

Chapter 14
Feelings (Willpower) and Fear.

"It's time to shift from being fear-driven to steward-driven."

"I don't feel motivated today." "What if I try and fail?" These are the two frameworks that many of us are accustomed to being guided by. Fear isn't always a bad thing, nor are your feelings. However, when they become the director of your day-to-day operations, delay and discouragement become inevitable. Why is that?

Time isn't something that we can get back, and we're only growing older. Let me tell you that you were placed here for a divine purpose, and your destiny awaits you. However, many of us don't allow ourselves to be developed because it requires discipline.

Unfortunately, discipline is something that most of us struggle with. We are on the struggle bus, where we become fixated on how we feel and make decisions from that place. If I don't feel like exercising today, then I won't do it. If I don't feel like doing my homework or this paper, then I won't do it. If I don't feel like cleaning up my house or folding my clothes, then I might not do it. If I make decisions solely based on how I feel, I will fall short because I am not allowing perseverance to grow, nor am I nurturing the disciplined version of myself.

On the flip side is the other F—Fear. If I fear stepping out of my comfort zone, I might not do it. If I am fearful of going to the doctor because of potentially bad news, then I might not do it. If I fear conversing with a loved one or my supervisor, I might not do it. If I am fearful of starting a business or starting a new relationship, then I might not do it. If I allow fear to be my guide, then grief is inevitable because I am losing out on the very experiences that were meant for me.

Sometimes we think we're doing ourselves a favor by not embarking on new adventures. However, if I never have it, I won't know what it feels like to lose it.

As a result, we may remain comfortable and complacent, not realizing that those opportunities are set-ups for lessons where growth is inevitable. Your destiny is contingent upon you growing through these challenges. Because each challenge, in essence, is a lesson. Your destiny encompasses you being the light in someone's darkness. Therefore, your lesson = light in somebody else's darkness and also highlights where you are meant to shine.

We often treat failure like it is final, but not knowing who you truly are and who you are meant to become is the real tragedy. Even Jesus said, "Lord, not my will, but your will be done." It is a daily choice to die to the false version of yourself and the part that is focused on temporary pleasures and comfort, to become more committed to the true version of yourself.

When you become more committed to the true version of yourself, transformation is inevitable; success is inevitable; growth is inevitable, and prosperity in every facet of your life is inevitable. To break the cycle of just going by your feelings, or your fear you need support and accountability. By aligning yourself with someone who has transcended the cycle, like a coach or mentor, progress becomes inevitable.

Investing in your progress may include:

- Healing from past hurts
- Forgiving those who have offended you
- Learning how to have healthy conversations
- Setting goals in a way that you can better achieve them.
- Understanding who you truly are.

It's time to shift from being fear-driven to steward-driven.

Being a steward means acknowledging that your life and everything that God has given you - family, house, car, talents, money, health, relationships, work, businesses, etc. - are under your supervision and need your commitment.

Dr. Myles Munroe said, “The wealthiest place in the world is not the gold mines of South America or the oil fields of Iraq or Iran. They are not the diamond mines of South Africa or the banks of the world. The wealthiest place on the planet is just down the road. It is the cemetery. There lie buried companies that were never started, inventions that were never made, bestselling books that were never written, and masterpieces that were never painted. In the cemetery is buried the greatest treasure of untapped potential."

What ideas or gifts do you currently possess that you have not acted upon? In the previous chapter, we talked about being easily distracted. However, studies show that mental focus and sharpness are best optimized when you are engaged in something that you are passionate about and genuinely care about. Many people become indistractable when they are doing something enjoyable, meaningful, and tied to an eternal purpose.

Dr. Myles Monroe put it like this: "True leaders are born when they find something to die for." I'm not saying that you have to become a martyr today, but what I am saying is that you are meant to be a leader and leave a legacy. There are ideas and dreams that you have that will create freedom for somebody else if you were to implement them. This also means that if you were to fail to implement them, you would be robbing somebody else of their freedom. Does it sound too harsh? That's okay, as long as the truth sets you free from analysis paralysis.

I can't stress this enough: time isn't something that we're going to get back, and we're only getting older. Let today be the day you begin to steward yourself and what God has given you well. Many of us want more but do not take care of what we currently have.

How am I going to sustain a healthy marriage if I don't invest in learning how to regulate my emotions and develop healthy conflict resolution? If I'm not a good manager of my bank account now, how am I going to manage billions or millions later? It's less about allowing your feelings or fear to guide you and more about making progress in each area of your life.

Progress leads to promotion and prosperity. Often, we disregard small beginnings in our quest for quick fixes. However, you cannot microwave mastery. It needs to cook. It needs to marinate. It needs to be nurtured. And it's in your investment and implementation of knowledge where you become a good steward. Remember, to whom much is given, much is required.

We often look at other people and compare ourselves to their progress and their transformation, not realizing that they made investments. They hired a coach. They hired a trainer. They hired someone who could support them and keep them accountable. If you want to break the cycle, you need to connect with someone who has transcended it and allow consistency and the true version of you to develop.

Many of us need a supportive push so that we can tap into the power and purpose that is dormant within. Do you need a push? Your transformation awaits you!

Exercise

List some of the dreams, ideas, or areas of your life that you want to make improvements in, and place them under “Optional” After that, create a new statement under “Must.”

Example:

Optional	Must
I made starting my coaching business optional because of fear	I must start my coaching business because I’m anointed for it, and others need my services

Optional	Must

Visit https://bonus.pure-ography.com/ to listen to the audio visualization.

Visualization

In this visualization, pick something you identified earlier that you want to be a good steward over. Visualize yourself in your room, and you hear a knock on the door. You open the door and it's God. He tells you that what you want to be a good steward over is actually something that He deposited in you before you were even born. He tells you that it is in you to be a good steward of it whether you already have it or are yet to implement it.

You now have a revelation that you are able to nurture and cultivate whatever He's given you and it will prosper. This stewardship was predestined since the dawn of time.

He then touches your head to show you what the future looks like because of your decision to commit today. Now, fast forward and envision yourself being a good steward over that very thing. Envision yourself having it and managing it well. Regardless of what it is, see yourself making progress and dominating.

What are the revelations you now have after this visualization?

Grab your mirror. It's time for affirmations

- I have it in me to win.
- There's a great plan that God has for my life.
- The dreams that God has given me need to be brought to life.
- I'm committed to being a good steward.
- I no longer despise small beginnings.
- I choose not to compare myself.
- I'm exactly where I ought to be.
- I commit to my purpose every single day.
- I'm committed to understanding my purpose.
- I'm committed to partnering with God.
- I permit myself to ask for help and invest in professional help.
- I make wise investments and I have great returns.
- I'm destined to have multiple streams of income.
- I am meant to be prosperous in my relationships.
- I'm committed to fostering healthy relationships with my family and friends.
- I am productive with my businesses.
- I am productive every single day.
- I have mastered how to relax.
- I'm committed to being debt-free.
- I use my wealth to create new memories for me and my family.
- I am committed to leaving a legacy.
- I'm committed to sharing my life.
- I am a good leader.
- I am driven by good stewardship.

Remember, winning is in your DNA. Your future self is depending on the decisions that you make today. Don't rob yourself of your blessing. Instead, rob the grave! Jesus came so that you can have life, and have it more abundantly. It is time to live. It is time to define your DNA!

Conclusion

Congratulations! You have just completed the 14-day mind purification journey. This is merely the beginning of the best chapters of your life, and I commend you for investing in your transformation. If you have identified that healing and transformation are needed, I encourage you to seek professional help.

Remember, you are a beacon of light and somebody else's darkness needs your illumination. We're all connected, and I've come to understand that "delaying my YES" in changing and answering the call would also be "delaying somebody's destiny." Remaining in the cycle not only affects you, but also affects your family, children, community, and everyone you're meant to help as well. The real tragedy isn't failure but knowing deep down that you're meant to make an impact and never answering the call. Say out loud, "NO MORE EXCUSES OR DELAYS!"

God delivered the children of Israel out of Egypt, freeing them from slavery. Yet, even on their journey, Egypt still lingered in their minds and it created hindrances and delays in their lives. It's time to get Egypt out of your mind for good so that you can stop barring yourself from your promised land. Peace and prosperity are yours in every aspect of your life. We often become our own obstacles, but not anymore.

Free will devoid of God's presence and lack of submission to the right leadership can lead us to remain in cycles and stagnancy. You don't have to keep running or walking in circles; connect with someone who has transcended the cycle, someone who is where you aspire to be so that you can get there as well You can reach me by booking a "Discover Your DNA" call at bonus.defineyourdna.com!

Finally, don't forget to check out the "Unleash Your Power and Purpose" interactive webinar! This isn't your average webinar. While creating it, I experienced the tangible presence of God. Yes, you read that right. The webinar is anointed. In this webinar, you will understand your barriers, identify what you need to break those limitations, and most importantly, you will gain insight into your calling and purpose! After investing in this webinar, you will embody the charge necessary to propel you toward your destiny. Visit the "Webinars" tab to begin today! https://define-your-dna.com

You can also visit www.define-your-dna.com to learn about all the services and products I offer.

I challenge you to explore who you are beyond the shadows of pain. Now is the time to truly discover who you are! I'm looking forward to connecting with you in the future!

www.ingramcontent.com/pod-product-compliance
Ingram Content Group UK Ltd.
Pitfield, Milton Keynes, MK11 3LW, UK
UKHW041852190726
13854UKWH00002B/858